Into the Old Town: walk 1

Start at the foot of **The Mound (pages 4–5)** and walk uphill to Edinburgh Castle by way of Mound Place and Ramsay Lane to Castle Esplanade.

Having explored **Edinburgh Castle (pages 6–7)**, stroll down Castlehill and **Lawnmarket (page 8)** before taking the steps at Upper Bow down to Victoria Street and **Grassmarket (page 9)**.

Go up Candlemaker Row to **Greyfriars Kirkyard (pages 10 –11)** before visiting the museum in Chambers Street. Turn left into South Bridge back to the Royal Mile. Turn right, exploring historic buildings in the High Street and **Canongate (pages 12–13)** before reaching **Holyrood (pages 14–15)**, where you will

Salisbury Crags in Holyrood **Park (page 16)** before walking back along Holyrood Road, turning right into St Mary's Street and left into the Royal Mile to reach Parliament Square and **St Giles' Cathedral (page 17)**. Follow St Giles Street and North Bank Street back to The Mound.

Around the New Town: walk 2

Starting at the Scott Monument in **Princes Street (pages 20–21)**, walk through West Princes Street Gardens and turn up Frederick Street and George Street to **Charlotte Square (page 22)**.

Head further into the New Town by way of Charlotte Street and Forres Street to **Moray Place and Royal Circus (page 23)**. Before climbing back uphill into **Queen Street and St Andrew Square (page 24)**, you might like to divert to quirky **Stockbridge (page 26)** and along the Water of Leith to the Royal Botanic Garden. Or you can take the free shuttle bus from the Scottish National Portrait Gallery in Queen Street to **Dean Village (page 25)** and its two outstanding galleries. A third option is to stroll from St Andrew Square along Waterloo Place and make the short climb up to **Calton Hill (page 27)**, before returning to Princes Street and your starting point.

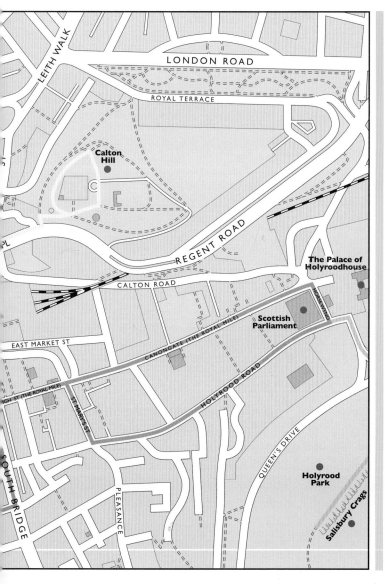

Welcome to Edinburgh

Built on centuries of struggle, shaped by extraordinary people and favoured with an unbeatable setting, Edinburgh has it all – history, romance, Scottish culture and tradition mixed with 21st-century charm and sophistication that lures visitors back time and time again. The skirl of the pipes, the tenements and dark closes of the Old Town's Royal Mile, dominated by the great grey mass of Edinburgh Castle, take you back centuries. The New Town's Georgian elegance is enhanced by the shops and cafés, restaurants, art galleries and green spaces.

Visitors travel the world to take part in Edinburgh's festivals of music, science, literature and the arts. This city of history and culture, excitement and art, has become one of the best-loved places in the world.

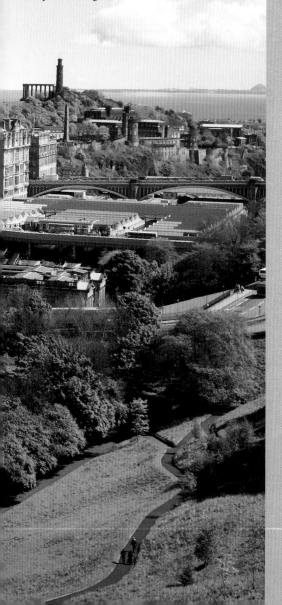

View from Edinburgh Castle

A short history

The volcanic rock on which Edinburgh Castle stands has been settled since the Bronze Age. Virtually unassailable on three sides, Din Eidyn, the fort on the hill, was key to controlling the region. In the middle of the 7th century AD, the Northumbrians took the high ground and changed the name to Edinburgh. King Malcolm III and his Queen, Margaret, made the castle their home in 1070 and future monarchs based themselves here. Their son King David I founded Holyrood Abbey in 1128 at the bottom of the rocky slope. The wars of independence followed with many battles against the English. Edward I, the 'Hammer of the Scots', sacked the castle in 1296. But in 1313 Scottish King Robert the Bruce ordered a daring raid on the castle – and won.

In the 15th century the capital of Scotland moved to Edinburgh. By the beginning of the 16th century Holyrood had become the preferred home of the Scottish royal family, and this was where the drama of Mary Queen of Scots was played out later in the century. The Act of Union in 1707 saw the dissolution of the Scottish Parliament and, after the crushing of the second Jacobite uprising in 1746, Edinburgh entered a period of peace and security in which the work of writers, thinkers and scientists flourished.

Overcrowding in what is now the Old Town became an urgent issue and in 1767 the building of the New Town was begun, based on architect James Craig's designs. The 20th century saw the founding of the Edinburgh Festival in 1947, while the acclaimed Museum of Scotland opened here in 1998. In 1999 Scotland regained its own parliament and the architecturally controversial Scottish Parliament building was opened in 2004, at the start of a new century of interest and excitement for this beautiful city of the north.

The Mound

As you stand at the foot of The Mound, you're between the old and the new. Until the mid 18th century the Old Town, a maze of narrow streets overhung by towering tenements and threaded with alleyways and closes, was where everyone lived and worked. Hard to believe, but beautiful Princes Street Gardens was the site of a stinking marsh, Nor'Loch, where everyone threw their rubbish. This was drained in 1759, in preparation for the building of the New Town and filled in with earth from the foundations of Princes Street.

Sir Henry Raeburn's 'Skating on Duddingston Loch'

National Gallery of Scotland

Two world-class galleries border an imposing piazza overlooking Princes Street Gardens. The National Gallery's collection of outstanding works of art is arranged in small rooms, so it is easy to choose what you want to see. Entry is free, making several short visits worthwhile. From the first-floor collection of 16th-century Italian painters to French Impressionists and Antonio Canova's *The Three Graces*, there's much to enjoy. The gallery's fragile collection of Turner watercolours is shown occasionally.

Royal Scottish Academy

Designed by William Playfair, as was the National Gallery with which it is linked, the Royal Scottish Academy has a regular programme of major art exhibitions.

National Gallery of Scotland and Royal Scottish Academy

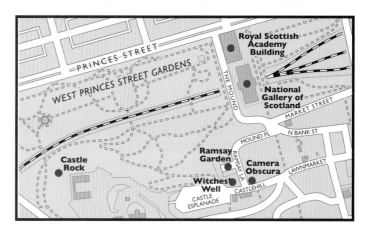

Castle Rock

Castle Rock is a long-extinct volcano, shaped over millions of years by the action of many layers of ice, in what is known as a 'crag and tail' formation. The volcano erupted 350 million years ago, cooling to become very hard rock. Over several ice ages, frozen water was forced around the hard plug – the 'crag' – carving out valleys where Princes Street Gardens now lie and forming a 'tail' of softer sedimentary rock (the Royal Mile and the Old Town) to the east.

Ramsay Garden

As you catch your breath on the hill, you'll see a cluster of distinctive red-and-white apartments looking across to the Firth of Forth. Ramsay Garden – named after Allan Ramsay (1686–1758), an Edinburgh poet who lived here – was built by enlightened town planner Sir Patrick Geddes in the 1890s.

White or black magic?

The panel on an iron wall fountain at the top of Castle Hill remembers 300 women burned here as witches. The good and evil faces, a snake and a foxglove, show the dual nature of witchcraft.

Camera Obscura and St Giles' Cathedral (see page 17)

Camera Obscura

This is not a modern idea, although there is much more to see than the basic projection of city views. You can look through rooftop telescopes, enjoy a gallery of illusions, holograms, 3D cityscapes and get a glimpse of Victorian Edinburgh. The first Camera Obscura was installed here in the 'Outlook Tower' in 1853, before Sir Patrick Geddes added an extra two storeys in 1892.

Edinburgh Castle

'*Nemo Me Impune Lacessit*' (roughly translated as 'No one may offend me and get away with it') is carved boldly above the great gatehouse into this impregnable fortress atop its craggy rock. These words warn off aggressors and give the clue that this castle has been at the centre of centuries of bitter and bloody struggle. It was last attacked in 1745 when Bonnie Prince Charlie unsuccessfully tried to regain the Scottish throne.

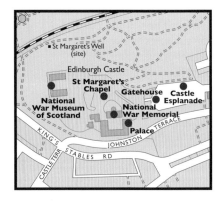

Castle Esplanade and Gatehouse

Here is the ceremonial parade ground, where the annual Tattoo takes place. The esplanade was built in 1753, probably as a tacit acknowledgement that hostilities were over. Two great leaders stand either side of the imposing gatehouse, entrance to a tunnel through the rock into the castle. They are William Wallace, who led Scottish resistance to the English occupation in the 13th century, and Robert the Bruce, who recaptured the castle from the English in 1313 – and promptly destroyed it so that it could not be taken again.

Gatehouse

The Palace

This is at the core of the cluster of buildings built high on the rock. Above the doorway are the entwined initials of Mary Queen of Scots and her second husband, Lord Darnley. You can visit the tiny room where Mary gave birth to James, the future king of both England and Scotland. There's often a queue to see the 'Honours', Scotland's crown jewels – the sceptre, the sword and the jewel-encrusted crown made for James V and incorporating Robert the Bruce's thin gold circlet – and the Stone of Destiny, on which early kings of Scotland are said to have been crowned.

Mons Meg

This huge siege gun fired stone cannonballs to nearly 1.5 miles (2.5 kilometres). When it was last fired in 1681, its barrel burst and it is now on display.

Big bang

At precisely one o'clock each day (Monday to Saturday) you'll hear a loud report echoing over the city. That's the famous one o'clock gun that you can watch being fired from the Mills Mount battery within the castle.

The Palace

Scottish National War Memorial

National War Museum of Scotland

Here are the lives of Scottish soldiers in battle. There are touching eve-of-battle letters, a locket containing hair belonging to soldier Sir John Moore, immortalized in Charles Wolfe's poem 'Not a drum was heard, not a funeral note …', and *The Thin Red Line*, the famous painting by Robert Gibb, showing the brave Highland Regiment at the Battle of Balaclava. Elsewhere in the castle you can learn about the Scots Dragoon Guards and the Royal Scots Regiment. The castle is the headquarters for the 52nd Infantry Brigade. The Scottish National War Memorial is in the old barracks which have been adapted to commemorate Scots who lost their lives in two World Wars.

St Margaret's Chapel

This 12th-century chapel was built by King David I to honour his mother, Queen Margaret, who was later canonized.

One o'clock gun

Lawnmarket and Grassmarket

These are the first two sections of the Royal Mile, which links Edinburgh Castle to Holyrood Palace. The backbone of the Old Town, narrow and steep at this end, is one of the world's most historic streets, where murderers and royalty have lived side by side with politicians and rich merchants. Grassmarket was once the haunt of thieves and bodysnatchers but is today a safe part of the city. You'll notice the change in street levels from the Royal Mile to Grassmarket, which is the result of glacial erosion.

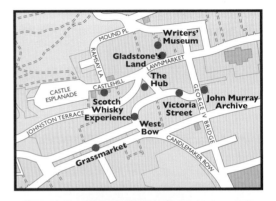

The Scotch Whisky Experience
Here a friendly ghost, a barrel-car ride through the history of whisky-making and a free dram teach you a lot about one of Scotland's best-known industries. If you like rare whiskies, you'll find them on sale here.

The Writers' Museum
This restored mansion, which once belonged to the exuberant society hostess Lady Stair, has been converted into a museum to celebrate the life and works of Robert Burns, Robert Louis Stephenson and Sir Walter Scott.

Gladstone's Land
This six-storeyed tenement house was the home of wealthy Thomas Gledstanes in the early 17th century. He altered the ground floor to create the arcaded stone front and lived on one of the floors, renting out the rest. Now the National Trust of Scotland has restored it so that you can visit the first two floors.

The Hub

The Hub
Look up at this impressive building where Castlehill meets Johnston Terrace. The spire, designed by Pugin, is the tallest in Edinburgh but it's not a church. Here is the colourful nerve centre and ticket office of the Edinburgh Festival in what was once the Assembly Hall for the Church of Scotland.

John Murray Archive

These letters and documents can be seen at the National Library of Scotland on George IV Bridge. Writers and thinkers such as Jane Austen, Charles Darwin and David Livingstone were all published by Murray, who kept correspondence and manuscripts. The archive includes the Byron Collection with the poet's letters to friends, family and mistresses.

Victoria Street

Victoria Street and West Bow

Although this attractive curving street is now lined with outstanding shops, restaurants and cafés, it was once part of the crime-ridden slum that much of the Old Town became in the 19th century.

Grassmarket

Grassmarket

This leafy square was a notorious part of the city in the days when bodysnatchers Burke and Hare murdered here to sell bodies for dissection. There were also public executions and the name of the pub, The Last Drop, is a grim reminder of those days.

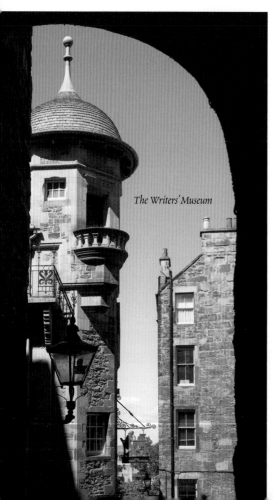

The Writers' Museum

Greyfriars Kirkyard

Here you can absorb so much Edinburgh history. Greyfriars Kirkyard is where notable Scots are buried – and where ordinary Scots stood shoulder-to-shoulder to defend their Presbyterian religion. It is mainly visited for its associations with sad little Greyfriars Bobby. Just across the road the outstanding National Museum of Scotland tells all about the country's culture, people, traditions and the land itself.

Greyfriars Bobby

If you have tears, prepare to shed them now. This small statue is of Bobby, a bright little Skye terrier who worked with his master, policeman John Gray. Gray died in 1858 and is buried in the kirkyard (churchyard) here. Bobby stood vigil over his master's grave for 14 years until death at last reunited them.

Greyfriars Bobby

Greyfriars Kirkyard

Greyfriars Kirkyard

Here in 1638 nobles, ministers and 5,000 townspeople lined up to sign the National Covenant, opposing Charles I's decision to impose the English prayer book and English bishops on the Scottish Church. The struggle went on for decades and you'll see a memorial to 1,200 Covenanters imprisoned here in 1679. Many died or were executed for their faith. One of the most magnificent tombs is that dedicated to the Adam brothers, great 18th-century architects. James Craig, designer of Edinburgh's New Town, is buried here too.

Nightlife

As you walk to the Royal Mile over South Bridge, look down to see the Cowgate area in the deep valley that leads from Holyrood to the Grassmarket. Many of the city's clubs are here and the area, deserted during the day, comes to life as the evening grows dark.

Lewis chessman

National Museum of Scotland

Enter this imposing sandstone building (completed in 1998) through a rounded tower to find a terrific series of exhibition spaces, starting at the beginning with a chunk of Lewisian gneiss, Scotland's oldest rock. Edinburgh sculptor Eduardo Paolozzi made the unusual bronze figures, each containing glass-fronted cases displaying early torques, necklaces, bracelets and brooches. There are treasure hoards, too, and you'll see the famous Lewis chessmen, carved from walrus tusks. Another Edinburgh artist, Andy Goldsworthy, has created a perfect slate wall and a whole whale skeleton arranged in a complete round. The museum's linked elegant Victorian building, with built-in fishponds, wrought iron and grand galleries, is a great place to spend an afternoon. Try to visit at a time when the extraordinary neo-Gothic Millennium Clock in the main hall is activated.

Eduardo Paolozzi's bronze figures, National Museum of Scotland

Canongate

You regain the Royal Mile over South Bridge, built between 1785 and 1788 over the deep valley that is Cowgate, making access to the city from the south easier for everyone. There is much to see in this part of the Royal Mile, which becomes less crowded and busy as you walk down the Canongate section towards Holyrood and the Scottish Parliament building.

Storytelling Centre

The Scottish Storytelling Centre and John Knox House

'Stories are told eye to eye, mind to mind and heart to heart' reads a panel in this most excellent space where not only children but adults too go to be entertained and informed. Open the cupboards in the Story Wall and press buttons to hear some of Scotland's most evocative tales. Groups can book storytelling sessions in the Bothy. The closely linked John Knox House, Edinburgh's oldest house, has an exhibition highlighting its famous inhabitants, although there is doubt whether John Knox himself spent much time here. The Storytelling Centre also houses the George Mackay Brown Library.

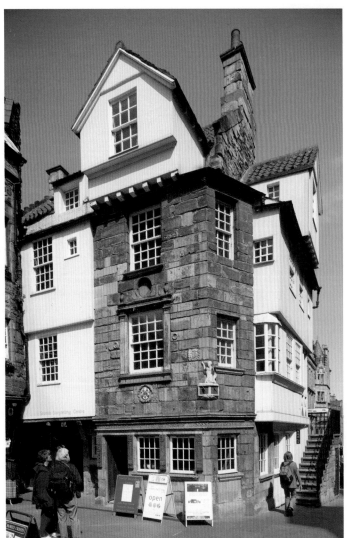

John Knox House

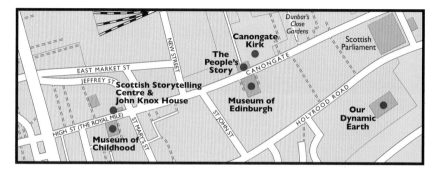

Advocate's Close

Closes, wynds and courts

Narrow passageways, sometimes leading to courtyard developments, sometimes acting as paths, lead off each side of the Royal Mile. You'll see inscriptions above many – Paisley Close bears the bust of a young man over the archway with the inscription: 'Heave awa' chaps, I'm no dead yet'. This is what the lad cried when a tenement collapsed and his rescuers sifted through the rubble. Dunbar's Close leads to a peaceful secret garden, while many, such as Advocate's Close, have views over the New Town.

Museum of Childhood

Here you have history and a nostalgic journey into your own, your parents' and grandparents' past. The dolls, teasets, teddies and train sets of years past have a rose-tinted glow, and you can find out about street games played by Edinburgh children in the 1950s. The museum, the brain child of town councillor Patrick Murray, a man who was said to dislike children, was opened in 1955.

Museum of Childhood

The People's Story and Canongate Kirk

In Canongate Tolbooth, variously a council office and a prison, you'll discover in vivid detail the tale of the ordinary people of the Old Town. Tableaux, recordings and display materials bring to life the tenement lifestyle of the people of Edinburgh over 200 years. Next door is Canongate Kirk, where poet Robbie Burns' muse 'Clarinda' (Agnes Maclehose) is buried.

Museum of Edinburgh

Everyday objects that tell the story of Edinburgh's local history are displayed here, including Greyfriars Bobby's collar and bowl.

Our Dynamic Earth

John Hutton, an 18th-century Edinburgh geologist, was the first to measure the timescale of Earth's evolution and this flamboyant building, with its re-creation of extraordinary natural phenomena, was constructed as a Millennium project in his honour.

Our Dynamic Earth

Holyrood

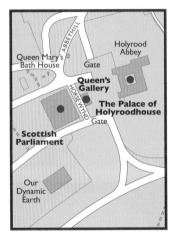

Here the ancient and modern stand side-by-side. The Palace of Holyroodhouse, to which the royal family decamped in the time of James II, is the old, while the Scottish Parliament, an imposing if sometimes challenging building, reflects the 21st century.

The Palace of Holyroodhouse

Holyrood Palace is a counterpoint to the great fortress of Edinburgh Castle, a mile up the hill. The palace was built in the grounds of ruined Holyrood Abbey, founded by King David I in 1128 after a hunting incident, so the story goes, when an attacking stag's antlers turned into a holy rood (a cross) and a divine command compelled him to build a monastery. The palace came later and the royal family moved from the often bleak castle to the much more comfortable surroundings of Holyrood. Today it is still the official royal residence in Scotland. The state apartments are open to the public, as are the older rooms once inhabited by Mary Queen of Scots – a chamber filled with her needlework and the tiny room where her jealous husband, Lord Darnley, ordered the fatal stabbing of David Rizzio as he played cards with Mary and her ladies.

Tragic queen

Queen at one week old, widow at 17, beautiful and talented Catholic Mary Queen of Scots married the selfish Lord Darnley in 1565. Their son, James, was born a year later, shortly before Darnley was murdered. Mary soon married the Earl of Bothwell, prime suspect in Darnley's death. This scandal forced her abdication and she was imprisoned for 19 years before her death warrant was signed by Queen Elizabeth I in 1587 when Mary was 44.

The Palace of Holyroodhouse

The Queen's Gallery

Here is an opportunity to see paintings from the Royal Collection in an outstanding building that is a work of art itself, made by craftsmen and women using natural materials imaginatively and decoratively. Opened in 2002 to celebrate HM the Queen's Golden Jubilee, it stands on the site of the Holyrood Free Church and the Duchess of Gordon's School. The arched stone entrance is decorated with carved garlands of wild flowers, including roses and thistles, while the doors have hinges shaped as branches of native trees – oak, chestnut, laburnum, rowan and hawthorn. The handles of the inner screen are sculpted figurines, and the curving wooden staircase is designed to represent people's legs.

The Queen's Gallery door

Scottish Parliament

This controversial £431m building, designed by Catalan architect Enric Miralles, is not a building you can ignore. It represents a harbour full of upturned boats and is either the most-loved or most-hated construction in Britain, depending on which poll you read. Miralles died before the building was completed. There's no admission charge to visit the public areas or the shop and café, but you pay for guided tours, which take place on most days. Outside the building you'll find food for thought in the sayings and quotes inscribed on the walls.

when we had a king and a chancellor and parliament men o'our ain, we could aye peeble them wi' stanes when they werena gude bairns – But naebody's nails can reach the length o' Lunnon.

Walter Scott

Scottish Parliament

Holyrood Park

Salisbury Crags and Arthur's Seat

As you start the winding walk up towards Salisbury Crags, passing sculptor Ronald Rae's *Lion of Scotland*, you'll find it hard to believe you're in the middle of a major European city. A craggy Scottish landscape, complete with hills, lochs and undulating moorland stretches before you.

Holyrood Park

Here are 650 rugged acres, topped by Arthur's Seat, an extinct volcano, rising to 254 metres (832 feet) and shaped like a crouching lion. The landscape was forged by volcanic activity more than 340 million years ago, and has been home to communities of people for 10,000 years. Here are four hill forts, seven holy wells and the remains of ancient hut circles.

Salisbury Crags

The path leading up to Salisbury Crags is known as the 'Radical Road' – it was built in 1820 by a group of unemployed weavers believed to hold radical views. The Crags were formed by volcanic eruption but are 25 million years younger than Arthur's Seat. From the towering rocks you can see Midlothian and the Borders to the south, the Firth of Forth to the west, Fife to the north, and the North Sea to the east.

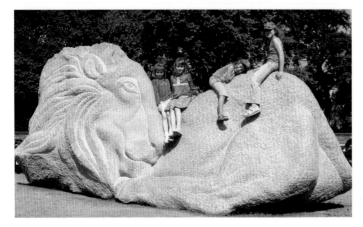

Rae's 'Lion of Scotland'

St Giles' Cathedral

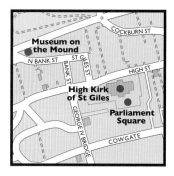

In this piazza you will find the High Kirk of St Giles, often called a cathedral, although it has no bishop. Tourists gaze at the imposing buildings, statues and monuments, while lawyers scurry across Parliament Square to the law courts.

St Giles' Cathedral, the High Kirk of Edinburgh

With its distinctive 'crown' steeple, St Giles', although mainly 15th century, stands where people have worshipped since at least AD 854. Inside are memorials to famous Scots, including Robert Louis Stevenson (reclining on a chaise longue), the Marquess of Montrose and his bitter enemy the 8th Duke of Argyll, both executed at the Mercat Cross, just outside. Don't miss Robert Lorimer's beautiful Thistle Chapel with its ornate carvings.

Money, money, money!

Museum on the Mound was opened in 2007 by HBOS plc to show the history of banking. Here you can see what one million pounds actually looks like and try to crack a safe.

Parliament Square

Parliament Square

This square was once the churchyard where John Knox, the zealous reformer, lies buried, although no one knows exactly where. The statue is of Charles II. Parliament House, the seat of the Scottish Parliament until it was dissolved in 1707, houses the High Court complex. The hall has an impressive hammerbeam roof and a massive stained-glass window.

Lucky heart

Don't tread on the Heart of Midlothian, a stone pattern in the ground in front of the High Kirk of St Giles. It marks the grim spot where the town prison once stood. Perversely, Scottish people spit on the heart for luck.

The Edinburgh Festival

The Edinburgh Festival is an umbrella term to describe the explosion of culture that takes over the city each August. The Edinburgh International Festival started in 1947 as a 'platform for the flowering of the human spirit'. Very soon other festivals sprang up alongside, notably the Fringe and the Edinburgh International Book Festival, the Edinburgh Jazz and Blues Festival and the Edinburgh International Film Festival. Today, the festival includes opera, ballet, music and theatre and the Military Tattoo – massed pipe bands in front of Edinburgh Castle – as well as the separate international festivals for books, jazz and blues, films and television.

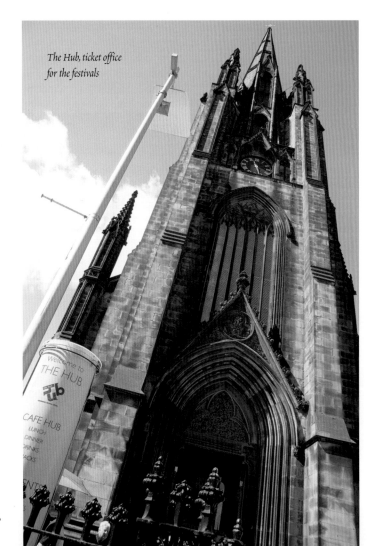

The Hub, ticket office for the festivals

Street performer

The Fringe

When the first Edinburgh Festival was launched, several theatre groups turned up uninvited, found themselves venues, and performed. A newspaper critic wrote about the excellent shows appearing 'around the fringes' of the official festival, and the Fringe was born. Now around 17,000 performers entrance or bewilder audiences at about 260 venues in the city each year.

The Fringe is the world's largest arts event, open to any performer organized enough to get to the city and find a venue. The shows embrace theatre, comedy, music, children's theatre, dance, exhibitions and events and many that don't easily fall into a

Comedy act, the Fringe

category. If you can't get tickets to see a show, you can enjoy watching one of the many street performers in Edinburgh during the summer.

Other events

The festival includes events hosted at other times of the year: a four-day celebration of Hogmanay at New Year, a Science Festival in April, a Children's Theatre Festival in May, and Mela (a multicultural celebration of the arts) in September.

Edinburgh Military Tattoo

Since it started in 1950, more than 12 million people have watched this spectacular and evocative performance played out on Castle Esplanade. Throughout August people gather as twilight falls in the narrow streets leading up to the castle. The floodlights are switched on as they take their seats and, as darkness spreads around the lighted area, the great oak doors of the castle are thrown open, the pipes and drums play and the massed bands march over the drawbridge. Music, dance and spectacular displays follow, until the show ends with a lone piper, outlined against the night sky, high on the castle ramparts, playing his haunting lament.

Edinburgh Military Tattoo

Princes Street

This long avenue, once an exclusive residential area, has one of the most famous views in the world. The shops line one side only so you look across the beautifully laid out gardens to the Old Town, whose skyline of spires, turrets and distinctive buildings is dominated by the great granite fortress that is Edinburgh Castle.

Scott Monument

Waverley Station is named after Sir Walter Scott's famous novel *Waverley*, published in 1814. Close to the station is the great man himself carved from marble, at the centre of what is said to be the largest memorial in the world to any writer. Scott, shown with his deerhound Maida, is surrounded by statuettes of his characters. The edifice reaches 61 metres (200 feet) and can be climbed by means of a spiral staircase.

Jenners

Jenners

Once the world's oldest independent department store (now part of a chain), this Edinburgh institution retains its unique character. Look up at the ornate exterior to see the female figures appearing to support the upper storeys – a tribute to all women who helped support its development by their purchases.

Scott Monument

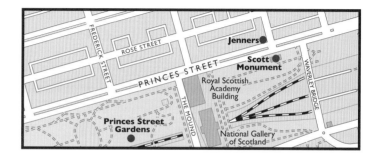

Princes Street Gardens

It is hard to believe that this area was once filled with a stinking mass of water, the Nor'Loch, created in 1460 as a defence for the Old Town. Everyone dumped their rubbish in it. But when the New Town was built, it was drained, filled in and a private garden created in 1818. The garden was opened to the public 60 years later. You can stroll, sit, enjoy a concert at the Ross Bandstand and admire the floral clock with its mechanical cuckoo. The gardens are sprinkled with monuments including ones commemorating explorer David Livingstone, publisher Adam Black, poet Allan Ramsay and the Royal Scots Greys. You'll hear the rumble of trains coming in and out of Waverley Station but you won't see them, thanks to a deep cutting.

Grand designs

There is a plaque inside the Royal Bank of Scotland in St Andrew Square marking the starting point of young architect James Craig's ambitious scheme for Edinburgh's New Town. The term 'New Town' is relative, as work started in 1767 when Craig won a competition to build 'another half' to a city that had become so crowded that life for many was uncomfortable. Other designers, including the Adam brothers, completed what Craig had started, building what became Europe's largest area of Georgian architecture.

Old Town skyline

Charlotte Square

A map of the New Town shows a neat grid with the two imposing squares, St Andrew Square in the east and Charlotte Square in the west. George Street is the spine, while Princes Street and Queen Street form the boundaries of architect James Craig's initial plan.

George Street

Take time to explore Rose Street and the other streets running parallel with George Street; they're full of interesting shops and historic 'howffs' (taverns), such as Milnes Bar in Rose Street. George Street itself runs atop a ridge and is lined with classy shops. The church of St Andrew and St George is oval (to prevent the devil from lurking in corners). At intersections you'll find grand statues and often unexpected views of Edinburgh Castle and the Firth of Forth.

Albert Memorial, Charlotte Square

The Georgian House

The Georgian House

The National Trust for Scotland has restored No. 7 in the style of its time, while across the square they run a café and small art gallery in No. 28.

Charlotte Square

This, the last part of James Craig's plan to be built, was designed by Robert Adam in 1791. Dominated by West Register House, where historic maps and plans are displayed, the square's palatial houses are imposing. The grassy park has at its centre the enormous Albert Memorial, showing him as horseman, husband, father and statesman. Queen Victoria was said to be so delighted with the piece that she knighted its sculptor, John Steell, without delay.

Moray Place and Royal Circus

The streets of the New Town are a joy to explore. Quiet, wide, elegant and harmonious, they are punctuated with green spaces. Most of the expensive properties are residential, but shops, bars and restaurants are opening up, making the area accessible to all. When you have explored these streets, you might like to visit the remarkable Stockbridge Colonies and the Royal Botanic Garden (see page 26).

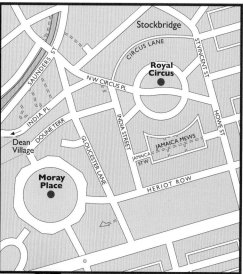

Moray Place

Moray Place

This glorious 12-sided Doric circus was, like Ainslie Place and Randolph Crescent to the south-west, the last and most imposing stage of the New Town development, built by the Earl of Moray in the three decades after 1822. The streets are cobbled, as in much of the New Town. The central gardens are private, while on the north side Moray Place Bank Gardens slope down to the Water of Leith. The Earl liked it so much he moved into No. 28.

Royal Circus

This grand circular development with a central garden, is linked architecturally to Great King Street and Drummond Place and was completed by 1820. Before you walk down India Street look into Heriot Row, where Robert Louis Stevenson lived at No. 17. No. 14 India Street, the International Centre for Mathematical Studies, was once the home of James Clerk Maxwell, the 'father of modern science'. A step away in Jamaica Street West is Kay's Bar, a tiny pub in the only remaining early 19th-century cottage in the street.

Taken for a ride

The corner of Great King Street and Dundas Street was where the last sedan chair was available for hire until 1870.

Queen Street and St Andrew Square

As you walk uphill towards Queen Street you might want to linger in Dundas Street, lined with art and antique shops of many types. Queen Street, with its private gardens, was the boundary of James Craig's original plan for the New Town.

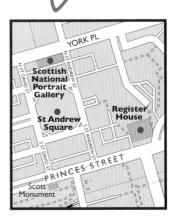

Sean Connery, National Portrait Gallery

Register House
The first domed building in Edinburgh, and one of Robert Adam's finest designs, this is the headquarters of the National Archives of Scotland.

St Andrew Square

Scottish National Portrait Gallery
You can't miss this ornate building, inspired by the Doge's Palace in Venice, because the red Dumfriesshire sandstone exterior, decorated with ornate figures, is in total contrast to the sober Georgian stone buildings around it. The figures include John Knox, Robert the Bruce and Adam Smith. Inside, William Hole's remarkable frieze of famous Scots lies below depictions of the battles of Bannockburn and Largs. Ground floor exhibitions change regularly, while the upper galleries tell Scotland's story from the perspective of its people.

St Andrew Square
This square is full of finance houses and a smart new shopping development. Walk inside the Royal Bank of Scotland to see the magnificent star-scattered domed ceiling. The tall column bears a statue of Henry Dundas, 1st Viscount Melville – Prime Minister William Pitt's right-hand man.

Dean Village

Part of the 12-mile (20-kilometre) Water of Leith Walkway runs through Edinburgh at Dean Village, passing the Scottish Gallery of Modern Art and the Dean Gallery. If you visit these galleries in Belford Road, it's worth strolling along the Water of Leith Walkway to the village, which is spectacularly set in a deep-sided gorge where the river once powered no fewer than 11 water mills.

Scottish National Gallery of Modern Art

Scottish National Gallery of Modern Art

There's plenty of room inside and out to display outstanding collections of modern art. Large pieces by Henry Moore, Rachael Whiteread, Barbara Hepworth and Ian Hamilton Finlay can be seen outside, but the most eye-catching is Charles Jencks dramatic *Landform Ueda*, occupying the lawn in front of the gallery. Children and adults alike enjoy pacing around the stepped serpentine mound reflected in crescent-shaped pools of water. Inside the gallery you'll find Matisse, Picasso, Bacon, Hockney, Warhol and Lucien Freud with more recent work by Antony Gormley, Damien Hirst, Tracey Emin and Gilbert and George.

Dean Gallery

Here is a world-class collection of Dada and surrealism and an internationally renowned permanent exhibition of pieces by Edinburgh-born sculptor Eduardo Paolozzi, whose distinctive postmodern sculptures may be seen in many places in the city centre.

Dean Cemetery

Occupying the grounds of Dean House, this graveyard contains some wonderful monumental work. Many prominent citizens of Edinburgh are buried here.

Jencks' 'Landform Ueda'

Stockbridge

Stockbridge, just 10 minutes walk from the city centre, is a sunny 'village' full of quirky shops and characters. It's an increasingly trendy part of the city, although it maintains its distinctive feel.

Troubled waters

The Water of Leith might seem a gentle river, trickling merrily through the north of the city, but residents living along its length know to their cost that it can swell hugely in the winter and flood houses and gardens.

St Stephen Street

Here you'll find an assortment of clothes and household shops, many open at odd hours and all worth browsing. Only the entrance remains of the old meat, fish and fruit market.

Royal Botanic Garden

You may enter this wonderful garden from Inverleith Row or Arboretum Place and enjoy its hillside setting. The café is a grand place to sit and enjoy the views over the city and across to the castle. This is a garden for all seasons, ablaze with rhododendrons and azaleas in spring, herbaceous plants and flowering trees in the summer and rich mellow tones in the autumn. Enthusiasts will enjoy the extensive alpine collection and everyone loves the enormous glasshouses.

Royal Botanic Garden

Symbols of the carpenter's craft

Stockbridge Colonies

Stockbridge Colonies

These 11 parallel cobbled cul-de-sacs of cottage-type houses were built by the Edinburgh Co-operative Building Company in the years following 1861. The idea was to provide low-cost housing for workers and, if you look at the gable-ends of the houses, you'll see carved panels depicting the different crafts.

Calton Hill

This surreal collection of monuments is the reason that Edinburgh was dubbed 'Athens of the North'. The half-finished, Grecian-style 'Parthenon' is William Playfair's National Monument, started in 1824 but left uncompleted when funds ran out in 1829. The energy expended in the short but steep climb is worth it not only for the extraordinary monuments, but also the fine views across the city in every direction.

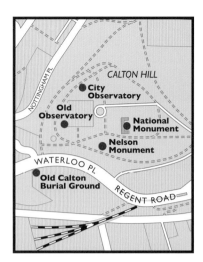

Old Calton Burial Ground

Before you climb the hill it's worth looking at these smaller scale monuments and the graves, including the huge Roman-style mausoleum designed by Robert Adam for philosopher David Hume, whose friends kept vigil here for eight nights after his burial in 1776 – to stop the devil coming for his atheist soul.

The monuments

The large telescope-shaped building is the 32-metre (106-foot) tower in memory of Lord Nelson, killed at the Battle of Trafalgar in 1805. The laying of the foundation stone in 1807 was kept a deep secret, in case crowds should attend and fall off the cliff. The other monuments, mostly designed by William Playfair, include a huge circular memorial to philosopher Dugald Stewart and the City Observatory next to the Old Observatory.

Nelson Monument

Long-standing vigil

The newest monument is a brazier-topped cairn put up to honour the men and women who kept vigil for 1,980 days from 10 April 1992 to 11 September 1997 as a stand for a Scottish Parliament. The cairn was erected in April 1998.

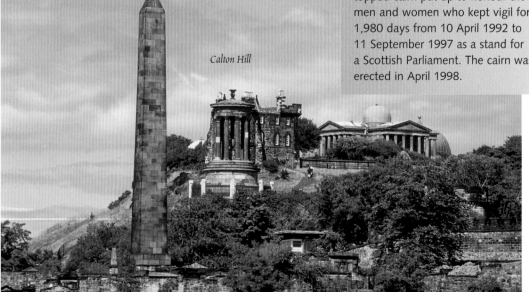

Calton Hill

Around Edinburgh

Although there is plenty to keep you entertained in Edinburgh, there are many interesting sights just a few miles from the city centre. Here are some of them.

Edinburgh Zoo

Conservation and environmental education are high on the agenda here and there is plenty for adults and children to see with more than 1,000 rare and beautiful animals in the zoo's 82 acres of parkland. The zoo is just 2.5 miles (4 kilometres) west of the city.

Queensferry

For 700 years a ferry carried people across the Firth of Forth between North and South Queensferry. In 1890, what was then the biggest bridge in the world – the Forth Railway Bridge – was opened and became one of the engineering wonders of the age. The Forth Road Bridge opened in 1964.

Cramond

This is the upmarket seaside village, north-west of the city centre, where Miss Jean Brodie's lover, Gordon Lowther, lived in Muriel Spark's lively novel *The Prime of Miss Jean Brodie*. Cramond is a pretty village with plenty of walks. In 1997 ferryman Rob Graham found the Roman sculpture of a

Cramond

lioness devouring a human. It was fished out of the River Almond and is now on show in the National Museum of Scotland in Chambers Street.

Leith

Edinburgh's ancient port, a short bus ride from the city centre, is where the former royal yacht *Britannia* is berthed. You can go aboard

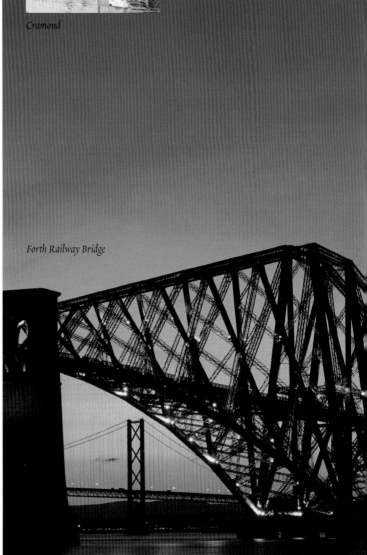
Forth Railway Bridge

Royal Yacht 'Britannia'

medieval castles in the country. The area around Craigmillar was once known as 'Little France' as Mary Queen of Scots, who grew up in France, often stayed here. The castle was almost certainly a base for those who plotted the murder of Lord Darnley, her husband.

and see where the Royal Family lived during 968 official voyages. Leith has a busy waterfront with smart shops, bars and restaurants.

Craigmillar Castle

Craigmillar, just 3 miles (5 kilometres) away from the city centre, is one of the most completely preserved

Rosslyn Chapel, Roslin

Everyone who has read religious 'conspiracy theory' books knows about this chapel, whose richly decorative carvings have led to speculation about its hidden secrets. Rosslyn Chapel in the village of Roslin, 6 miles (9.5 kilometres) to the south of Edinburgh, was built by William St Clair, Prince of Orkney, in 1446. There's a carving of him inside, with stars and cockle shells around his head. Look for the 'apprentice pillar' said to have been accomplished by a trainee while the master mason was away. Legend says the mason returned and, jealous at the beauty of the carving, killed the boy. A carved head with a great wound represents this sad story.

Rosslyn Chapel

Information

Full up-to-date information on walks, trips, tours and what to see and do in Edinburgh may be found at the Tourist Information Centre.

Tours and trips

Information on the following and many other tours may be found at the Tourist Information Centre or on www.edinburgh.org.

The many (and often scary) themed walking tours include: City of the Dead, Cadies and Witchery Tour, Auld Reekie Tours, Mercat Tours, Rebus Tours, Geowalks, Leith Walks, Edinburgh Literary Pub Tour.

Open-top bus tours provide hop-on-and-off rides around the city and depart regularly from Waverley Bridge. You can buy a ticket from the booth by the bridge, or on the bus.

Non-strenuous cycle tours around the Old and New Town last about 3 hours.

Tourist bus

Museums, galleries and historic sites

Camera Obscura 0131 226 3709, www.camera-obscura.co.uk;
Dean Gallery 0131 624 6200, www.nationalgalleries.org;
Dynamic Earth 0131 550 7800, www.dynamicearth.co.uk;
Edinburgh Castle 0131 225 9846, www.edinburghcastle.biz;
The Georgian House 0844 4932118, www.nts.org.uk;
Gladstone's Land 0844 4932120, www.nts.org.uk;
Museum of Childhood 0131 529 4142, www.cac.org.uk;
Museum of Edinburgh 0131 529 4143, www.cac.org.uk;
Museum on the Mound 0131 243 5464, www.museumonthemound.com;
National Gallery of Scotland 0131 624 6200, www.nationalgalleries.org;
National Library of Scotland 0131 623 3700, www.nls.uk;
National Museum of Scotland 0131 247 4422, www.nms.ac.uk;
National War Museum of Scotland 0131 247 4413, www.nms.ac.uk/war;
The Palace of Holyroodhouse 0131 556 5100, www.royalcollection.org.uk;
The People's Story 0131 529 4057, www.cac.org.uk;
The Queen's Gallery 0131 556 5100, www.royal.gov.uk;
Royal Botanic Garden 0131 552 7171, www.rbge.org.uk;
Royal Scottish Academy 0131 624 6200, www.nationalgalleries.org;
Scottish National Gallery of Modern Art 0131 624 6200, www.nationalgalleries.org;
Scottish National Portrait Gallery 0131 624 6200, www.nationalgalleries.org;
Scottish Parliament 0131 384 5200, www.scottish.parliament.uk;
The Scottish Storytelling Centre and John Knox House 0131 556 9579, www.scottishstorytellingcentre.co.uk;
The Scotch Whisky Experience 0131 220 0441, www.scotch-whisky-experience.co.uk;
The Writers' Museum 0131 529 4901, www.cac.org.uk

Art galleries' shuttle bus

Index of places

Gladstone's Land

Visit Scotland Tourist Information Centre ℹ
3 Princes Street,
Edinburgh EH2 2QP
tel: 0845 2255 121
website: www.edinburgh.org

Shopmobility ♿
For the loan of powered wheelchairs and electric scooters for those with limited mobility.
St Andrew Square
To book, tel: 0131 225 9559

Ghost Fest held in May

Front cover: Edinburgh
Castle
Back cover: Scottish dancers

Acknowledgements
Photography © Pitkin Publishing
by Neil Jinkerson. Additional
photography by kind permission
of: Alamy: FC (KCphotography),
23cl (Ange), 19l, 27b (Robert
Harding Picture Library), 26cr
(Stock Images), 28/29 (BL
Images Ltd), 29t (Colin Palmer
Photography), 29cr (Stuart
Walker), 30t (Bernie Pearson);
Bridgeman Art Library: 4t
(National Gallery of Scotland),
14cl (Victoria & Albert Museum,
London); Epic Scotland: BC
(Ashley Coombes); National
Museum of Scotland: 11cl;
National Trust for Scotland: 22bl;
Nicko and Joe's Bad Film Club:
19t; Our Dynamic Earth
Enterprises Ltd: 13br; Scottish
National Portrait Gallery: 24tl.

The publishers would like to
thank Linda Galt of Visit
Scotland for her assistance in the
preparation of this guide.

Written by Annie Bullen; the
author has asserted her moral
rights.
Edited by Angela Royston.
Designed by Simon Borrough.
Additional picture research by
Jan Kean.
Maps by The Map Studio Ltd,
Romsey, Hants, UK; maps based
on cartography © George Philip
Ltd.

Publication in this form © Pitkin
Publishing 2008.

All information correct at time
of going to press, but may be
subject to change.

Printed in Great Britain.
ISBN 978 1 84165 213 9   1/08

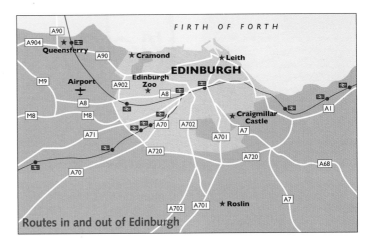

Routes in and out of Edinburgh

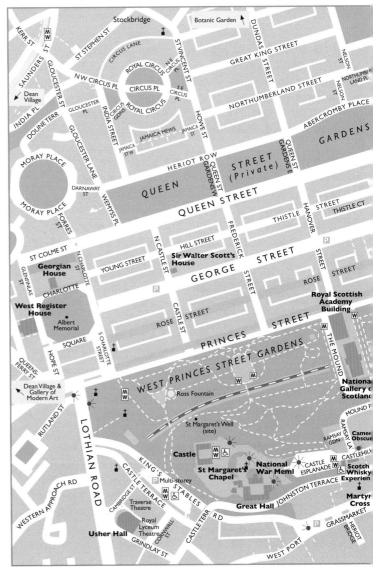